W9-AYO-145

J          $8.95
921        Deegan, Paul J
De            Michael Jordan,
           basketball's
           soaring star

## DATE DUE

| | | | |
|---|---|---|---|
| FE 14 '91 | JY  9 '92 | SEP 1 90 | JUL 27 98 |
| MR  8 '91 | JY 31 '92 | NOV 1 5  94 | AG 18 00 |
| MR 30 9   | OC   1 '9 | FEB 0 2  95 | FE 05 '02 |
| AP 25 '91 | OC   1 '92 | MAY 1 6   | AG 12 '02 |
| JE  7 '91 | FE 26 '9  | FEB 1 0  98 | NO 19 02 |
| AG 02 '91 | AP 27 '9  | FEB 2 9  96 | MR 0 4 '04 |
| AG 19 '91 | JE 28 '93 | JUN 07   98 | JY 08 05 |
| NO 27 '91 | JY  8 '93 | SEP 0 9  98 | JY 20 '05 |
| DE 11 '91 | OC  2 '9  | FEB 1 7  | FE 2 7 '77 |
| FE 12 '92 | JAN 98 94 |  | |
| MR 19 '92 | JUN 3 0  94 | FEB 1 7 | JY 06 77 |
| JE 23    94 | AUG 1 5  94 | JUL 0 8 98 | OC 1 1 '77 |

EAU CLAIRE DISTRICT LIBRARY

DEMCO

# MICHAEL JORDAN

# MICHAEL JORDAN

## Basketball's Soaring Star

**Paul J. Deegan**

EAU CLAIRE DISTRICT LIBRARY

Lerner Publications Company ■ Minneapolis

Apple Book 12/26/90 #8.25

81694

*This book is available in two editions:*
Library binding by Lerner Publications Company
Soft cover by First Avenue Editions
241 First Avenue North
Minneapolis, Minnesota 55401

**To Dorothy, my best friend**

LIBRARY OF CONGRESS CATALOGING-IN-PUBLICATION DATA

**Deegan, Paul J. 1937-**
Michael Jordan: basketball's soaring star.
(The Achievers)
Summary: Describes the life and career of the Chicago
Bulls basketball player who became the first player in
twenty-four years to score more than 3,000 points in one
season.
1. Jordan, Michael, 1963- —Juvenile literature. 2.
Basketball players—United States—Biography—Juvenile
literature. 3. Chicago Bulls (Basketball team)—Juvenile
literature. [1. Jordan, Michael, 1963-   . 2. Basketball
players. 3. Afro-Americans—Biography] I. Title. II. Series.
GV884.J67D44  1988  796.32'3'0924 [B] [92]  87-29669
ISBN 0-8225-0492-8 (lib. bdg.)
ISBN 0-8225-9548-6 (pbk.)

Copyright © 1988 by Lerner Publications Company

All rights reserved. International copyright secured. No part of
this book may be reproduced or transmitted in any form or by any
means, electronic or mechanical, including photocopying and
recording, or by any information storage or retrieval system,
without permission in writing from the publisher, except for the
inclusion of brief quotations in an acknowledged review.

Manufactured in the United States of America

International Standard Book Number: 0-8225-0492-8 (lib. bdg.)
International Standard Book Number: 0-8225-9548-6 (pbk.)
Library of Congress Catalog Card Number: 87-29669

5  6  7  8  9  10  98  97  96  95  94  93  92  91  90

# Contents

1 Records Lead to Recognition . . . .  7

2 Overcoming Disappointment . . .  17

3 The Jordan Family . . . . . . . . . . .  27

4 Jordan and the NBA . . . . . . . . .  33

5 Sharing His Success . . . . . . . . . .  45

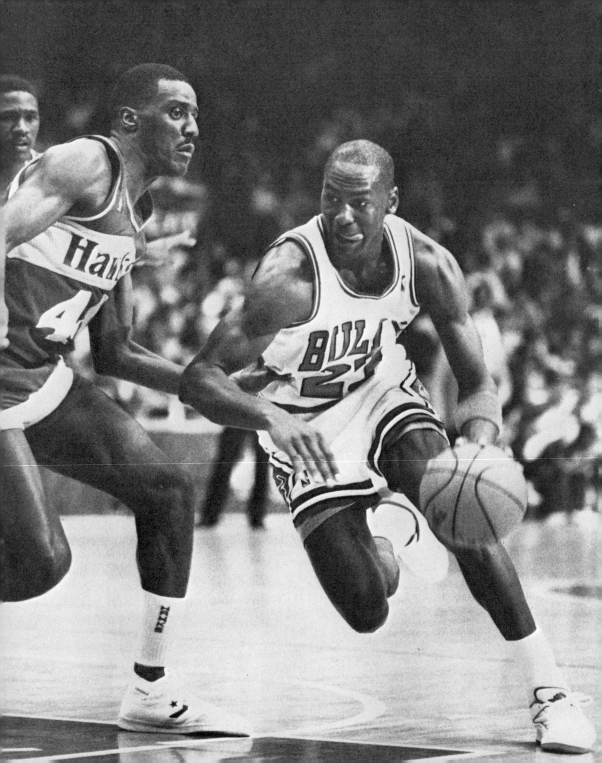

# 1

# *Records Lead to Recognition*

One of the most exciting scenes in sports today is basketball player Michael Jordan of the Chicago Bulls preparing to shoot a basket. Ball in hand, eyes narrowed in concentration, his tongue hanging out, Jordan becomes a devastating weapon. He can dart past a defensive player in a flash or outjump him and score the basket. His speed and jumping ability are just two of Jordan's many assets, which include his size, strength, control, large hands, and durability. The 6-foot, 6-inch guard with the acrobatic leaping ability is fast on his way to becoming one of the all-time greats of the National Basketball Association (NBA).

Michael Jordan is considered one of the best players in the NBA today. During the 1986–87 season, he scored 3,041 points, the third highest total in NBA history after Wilt Chamberlain's two highest scoring totals. Jordan was the first player in 24 years to score more than 3,000 points in one season. Until Jordan averaged 37.1 points a game in the 1986–87 regular season, no NBA guard had ever averaged more than 34 points in a game.

Bobby Knight, considered one of the country's most successful college coaches, called Jordan one of the two best college players he's seen in the last 10 years. Larry Bird, the Boston Celtics' famous forward and three-time NBA Most-Valuable-Player award winner, said Jordan "can do things that nobody else does in this league. He's got everything."

Many people think Bird is the best player in basket-ball today. But Bird says, "Jordan can do a lot of things that I can't do. I can't jump like him. I can't run like him. I can't just go over people to get to the bucket. Never seen anyone like him. Phenomenal. One of a kind. He's the best ever."

Jordan makes it seem simple. He says the moves for which he is becoming famous in arenas across the country are spontaneous. "The special shots are alternatives after the defense makes me change the normal shot," Jordan has said. "I can't plan what I'm doing because I don't know what the defender is going to do."

That spontaneity makes Jordan a tough opponent. A defensive player has no idea what Jordan might do next. His many abilities make him hard to defend against.

Even when defenses make him change his shot, Jordan has a knack for getting the ball off in traffic.

Jordan's very large hands, which can wrap a basketball, are an
asset to him on the court.

At 195 to 200 pounds, he is very strong and is not easily bumped around. His great body control and agility enable him to shoot successfully in tight situations.

Jordan's very large hands make it easy for him to control the ball, switch the ball from hand to hand, and grasp the ball firmly when he flies toward the hoop. His large hands also allow him to fake a pass, then pull the ball back and bypass a defender.

Many observers have noted Jordan's almost uncanny ability to stay in the air for a long time when he leaps for a basket. Basketball players call this time in the air "hang time." Jordan appears at times to hang forever. One reporter said that Jordan "seems to float in midair and wait for other men to fall to earth before he shoots."

Jordan's first coach with the Bulls, Kevin Loughery, compared Jordan's hang time to that of all-time NBA great Julius Erving—"Dr. J." "Players with great hang time," Loughery said, "can stay up there when they jump in the air." He added that they can "get their bodies into different positions in the air."

Erving, after playing against Jordan for the first time, said, "In some ways, it's like looking into a mirror." Erving called Jordan's playing "something magical or mystical." Jordan said he was flattered to be compared with Dr. J, but he added, "He [Erving] made his own footsteps, and I don't want to follow in his. I want to make my own—size 13."

After opponents drop out of his way, Jordan, still in midair, is often able to score.

12

Jordan shares one physical skill with nearly all other great athletes—foot speed and overall quickness. Jordan's powerful first step catapults him into his remarkable drives to the basket, often followed by a slam dunk. Most players at the major college and professional levels can dunk the ball, but Jordan can do it by leaping higher than a 7-foot player is able to. It takes tremendous strength to jump higher than players six inches taller can jump.

The mere presence and personality of a player like Jordan lend a special quality to a basketball game. Stan Albeck, Loughery's successor as the Bulls' coach, said, "It's not only his scoring, it's his presence. He makes everyone play harder. He gets the crowd—everyone—involved." One observer of the Bulls said Jordan's ability sometimes made team members "believe they were better than they really were."

Jordan has also proved durable, playing despite colds, flu, and other nagging pains that plague a player during the six-month NBA season. Chicago assistant coach John Bach said, "That's what makes it so nice to be with the Air Jordan airline. It flies every night."

The ability to inspire teammates and durability are important, but in the end it's Jordan's great physical talent that is so exciting. Professional athletes are not easily impressed, but even NBA players admire Jordan. "Leave him alone. He's God's child," a Bulls' teammate told reporters.

EAU CLAIRE DISTRICT LIBRARY

Jordan's powerful first step, here moving him past the Boston
Celtics' Kevin McHale, often frees him for a slam dunk (right).

Jordan is modest about his abilities. "It's all spur-of-the-moment," he said. "If I'm in a situation where I have to do something spectacular to get out of trouble, I do it. The new moves come in as they come. It's nothing that I think about before I do it. Sometimes I don't know exactly what to do, but I end up doing it."

His talents are readily acknowledged by many in the sports world, though. Former Notre Dame star Orlando Woolridge entered the NBA three years before Jordan. Woolridge said that several elements distinguish an excellent player. "You look to see what type of things he can do instinctively, what his natural ability is, and what types of things he can do in certain pressure situations. It's easy to judge who's a good shooter, who's a good defender, who rebounds well," Woodridge said. "But a player who can do all those things, especially in pressure situations, is the type of player I look for." Woolridge said he was talking about a player "who can do the whole thing," one "with pure natural ability. A man like Michael Jordan."

# 2

# *Overcoming Disappointment*

Jordan didn't begin his basketball career with the ability to do "the whole thing," however. Reaching basketball stardom was not a smooth, uninterrupted climb. His success reflects a pattern of growth that developed gradually—both on and off the basketball court. The heart of Jordan's story centers on how he succeeded in combining his strong competitive instinct with his emerging physical talent—a talent that was not so evident when he began playing high school basketball. Even after three years in one of the most successful college basketball programs in the country, no one expected Jordan to become the red-hot NBA property he is today.

Jordan committed himself to basketball only after it disappointed him. Although he had begun playing basketball as a child at an eight-foot-high basket in his backyard, his athletic skills were not obvious in his first years at Laney High School in Wilmington, North Carolina. As a sophomore at Laney in 1979, he averaged 25 points a game on the junior varsity team, and he expected a promotion to the varsity team. It never came.

Jordan responded by meeting the challenge. "The way it is in our family," his father said, "is that we try to make something happen rather than waiting around for it to happen. We believe the surest way is to work toward making it the way you want."

During the summer of 1979, Jordan turned himself into a "gym rat," practicing basketball for hours at a time. He even cut back on baseball, which had been his favorite sport, to devote more time to improving his basketball game.

His persistence paid off. Jordan made the varsity basketball team, and, by the time he was a senior, he'd become a strong player. He was no nationally sought-after schoolboy star, though. He was just one of many good high school basketball players in North Carolina. Most of his advisers urged Jordan to attend a small college in North Carolina where, they thought, he'd have more opportunity to play. Jordan saw the situation as another challenge. He chose to go to the University of North Carolina at Chapel Hill and try to succeed in one of the best major college basketball programs in the country.

Jordan began playing basketball at a basket only 8 feet high.
Now he plays above the rim of the regulation 10-foot-high basket.

And succeed he did as his growth continued. Coach Dean Smith said Jordan's progress at North Carolina was "eerie." During Jordan's three seasons with the Tar Heels, he became much more than just an average college player—he became an exceptional college player.

North Carolina Coach Dean Smith

As a college player, Jordan is best remembered for one shot he made in his first season at North Carolina. He made a 16-foot shot in the closing seconds of the 1982 National Collegiate Athletic Association (NCAA) championship game. The freshman's successful shot gave the Tar Heels a 63–62 win over Georgetown University.

A few years later, Jordan told a reporter that the 1982 championship game was his one "memorable game," noting that "everything started with my [winning] shot. That's the game I will always remember because that's when Michael Jordan got his name and started to get the respect of everyone else."

Jordan was named an All-American player and College Player of the Year in his sophomore and junior years. In his sophomore year, the Tar Heels went as far as the regional final before falling to the University of Georgia, 82-77. Jordan—listed then and the following year as 6 feet, 5 inches tall—averaged 19.1 points on 53.5 percent field-goal shooting in 1982-83. He scored 687 points and had over five rebounds a game.

As a junior in his final year at Chapel Hill, Jordan led the Atlantic Coast Conference (ACC) in scoring as North Carolina went undefeated in the conference. For the season, he averaged 19.6 points a game, making 55 percent of his field-goal attempts. Seventy-eight percent of his free throws were successful. He scored 607 points and averaged over five rebounds per game. The team's bid for another NCAA title ended in a regional semifinal game that Indiana University won, 72-68.

At Chapel Hill, Jordan learned something about basketball fans. He realized that they expected great things of him. "They're going to want me to [spin] 360 [degrees] each time I've got the ball," Jordan said. "But [now] I know if I just go out and play naturally, the people are going to be pleased." At the beginning of his final season at Chapel Hill, he said he was "trying to do it for the crowd." But he wasn't playing well. Coach Smith then showed him films of games from the previous year. "The difference was incredible," Jordan said. "From that point on, I just settled down and started to play the way I normally do, and it worked out."

Despite Jordan's impressive college record, there was still no indication of how much he would affect the NBA—an entire league of outstanding players. In particular, Jordan did not often display his unique aerial abilities at North Carolina because coach Smith's carefully constructed offensive plans did not emphasize an individual player's physical talents.

As a member and co-captain of the 1984 United States Olympic basketball team, Jordan played for a coach with a similar offensive approach. Indiana University coach Bobby Knight was not about to let a member of his team show off on the court.

Orlando Woolridge, Jordan's Chicago Bulls team-mate, compared playing college sports to playing in an orchestra: The coach is the conductor, and players must play the music according to the coach's directions. "If you don't play the right notes, you sit down," Woolridge said. "When you get to the pros," he continued, "it's more like jazz. . . . You can just play and let your rhythm flow, do the things that come naturally and let your talent show." Coach Knight wasn't conducting jazz. However, Jordan did average just over 17 points a game in the Olympics as he led the U.S. team to a gold medal in Los Angeles.

A coach's style can limit a college player's flair. Still, Michael Jordan of the Bulls is a much more explosive player than the Michael Jordan of North Carolina and Olympic days. Jordan thinks it just took time for him to hit his stride. "In college the natural skills and ability were there, but it was a learning experience for me," he noted. "At the pro level . . . all my knowledge and ability just came together. I came to a team where the situation gave me an opportunity to show the world what I can do as a player."

In 1987, he told a reporter that "the NBA is an educational playground. It's allowed me to combine all I've learned about fundamentals with my natural skills." That combination, along with his strong competitive drive, produced immediate results when Jordan entered the NBA.

The decision to go to North Carolina may have seemed risky, but it worked out well for both Jordan and the University's basketball program. Although Jordan left school after his junior year for the challenges and riches of professional basketball, he also returned to college periodically and received his degree in 1986.

Chicago Bulls' ex-coach Doug Collins has expressed surprise at Jordan's ability to maintain "mountains of freshness."

# 3

## *The Jordan Family*

Growing up in Wilmington, North Carolina, Jordan often felt unpopular and awkward. Although admired today by many fans, as a boy Jordan was convinced he was so ugly that he would never get married. Other kids made fun of him, and, when he got to high school, he rarely dated.

Despite his lack of self-confidence as an adolescent, Jordan today shows a healthy personality that stems from the warmth and care given to him by his family. Through their encouragement, he was able to develop the strength necessary to succeed on and off the basketball court. Today Jordan is himself both a husband and a father. In September 1989, Jordan married Juanita Vanoy, and the couple has a young son named Jeffrey.

Michael Jordan was born in Brooklyn, New York, on February 17, 1963. Shortly after his birth, his parents,

James and Dolores Jordan, moved their family to Wallace, North Carolina, James' hometown. Michael, the second youngest of five children, had two brothers and two sisters. When he was seven years old, the family moved to Wilmington. James was a plant supervisor for General Electric, and Dolores worked in public relations for a banking firm.

A friend of the family describes Dolores Jordan as "the strong one in the family" and "the disciplinarian, the steadying influence." Michael says his mother is "the one who always told me to respect my elders." Michael's father is called "fun-loving and easygoing," with "a streak of mischief that you also can see in Michael." He is also "a man who lives by the work ethic."

When Michael was young, his brothers enjoyed working with cars, appliances, radios—things they could fix. Michael, though not mechanically inclined, watched his father repair many things in their garage workshop. In those work sessions Michael picked up the habit of letting his tongue hang out while concentrating, as he saw his father do.

Michael also helped his mother in the kitchen. Since he was sure no one would marry him, he decided that he should be able to take care of himself so he could live alone someday. He asked his mother to teach him to cook, to wash clothes, to clean house, and to sew. Jordan says he was "lazy about some things" when he was growing up. "I never got into mowing the lawn or doing hard jobs. But I wasn't careless."

Dolores and James encouraged their children to excel at whatever they did. "My parents warned me about the traps [in life]," Jordan says, "the drugs, and the drink, the streets that could catch you if you got careless." Although his parents did not push Jordan toward athletics, he participated in baseball, football, and track. He says he was "trying to find the right place for my talents."

He liked baseball the most when he was growing up. "My favorite childhood memory, my greatest accomplishment," Jordan told a reporter, "was when I got the most-valuable-player award when my Babe Ruth team won the state baseball championship. That was the first big thing I accomplished in my life, and you always remember the first." Jordan treasures that championship even more than the NCAA title his North Carolina team won.

James Jordan says Michael's competitive drive comes from his mother. Michael's urge to compete extends beyond the basketball court. He hates to lose—at anything.

Jordan is competitive, but he can be warm and caring as well. He tries to be fair. During training camp for the Bulls in 1985, on a day off, Jordan began shooting pool. He played with anyone who would challenge him—five dollars a game. He beat everyone and was having a good time. He talked and laughed and jived as he played his shots, which intimidated some opponents.

One 10-year-old boy was more confident, however. The youngster, an unusually keen sharpshooter, was holding his own in a close game with Jordan. Jordan won. When Jordan asked for the five dollars, the boy lowered his head and dug into his pocket. He'd obviously thought that Jordan wouldn't make him pay if he lost. But Jordan told the boy that if he were going to gamble in life, he'd better be willing to pay the price when he lost.

Then during the next game, Jordan asked the boy to rack the balls for him, offering him five dollars to do it. The youngster seemed to appreciate the opportunity to earn back his losses, and he walked away with a smile. His faith in the fairness of a sports hero had deepened.

Tongue out, Jordan soars to the basket.

# 4

# *Jordan and the NBA*

In the spring of 1984, Jordan was the first-round choice of the Chicago Bulls, the third player picked in the NBA draft. That fall, Jordan got off to an outstanding start with the Bulls, scoring 22 points in one quarter during his third regular-season game and totaling 45 points in his ninth NBA game. Chicago won three straight games on the road for the first time in three years.

Playing in every one of the Bulls' 82 regular-season games in 1984–85, Jordan led Chicago into the play-offs for the first time in four seasons. They met the central division champion, the Milwaukee Bucks, in the first round of the play-offs and were eliminated three games to one.

Jordan's scoring average of 28.2 points a game was third best in the NBA behind established stars Bernard

Bernard King of the New York Knickerbockers averaged 32.9
points per game to lead the NBA in scoring in 1984-85. He
missed almost all of the next 2 seasons after suffering a devastating knee injury in March, 1985. The 6-foot, 7-inch forward was
traded to the Washington Bullets just before the 1986-87 season.

King of the New York Knickerbockers and the Celtics' Larry Bird. While scoring 2,313 points, Jordan made over half of his field-goal attempts. His 2.39 steals a game was fourth best in the league.

One basketball publication asked, "Could anyone have done more in his rookie year?" His performance brought Jordan NBA Rookie-of-the-Year honors and a spot on the all-NBA team. A television announcer said Jordan "did everything except make the wind stop blowing in Chicago." He received 74 percent of the votes cast for Rookie of the Year and was named NBA Pivotal Player of the Year, an award that rates a player's overall value to his team.

The rookie Jordan also revitalized the Chicago Bulls' organization. Thousands of fans lined up to see Jordan. During games, they waited eagerly for him to make a move to the basket. With his tongue hanging out, he would soar to the basket. The fans loved to watch him dunk the ball through the rim.

NBA commissioner David Stern said that Jordan's impact on the league was "tremendous, more than anyone expected." One NBA team's marketing direc- tor called him "the Bruce Springsteen of the NBA" because of his tremendous crowd-drawing power. During Jordan's first year in Chicago, attendance at Bulls games almost doubled over the previous season. Ticket sales rose 87 percent from an average of 6,365 fans per game to 11,887. Bulls games even sold out in attendance-poor cities like Oakland and Cleveland. The Bulls were one of seven NBA teams to draw over a million fans in combined home and road games in 1984–85. "I expected a warm reception in Chicago," Jordan said, "but as for those crowds on the road, I can't explain how good it feels to hear those cheers."

Jordan's popularity and his chemistry with fans were displayed even before his first official NBA game. The Chicago rookie was mobbed by screaming teenage girls at an exhibition game in nearby Gary, Indiana. After another exhibition game, a woman who had been unable to obtain Jordan's autograph lay down in front of the car that was carrying him. She refused to move. "I don't care if you run over me," she said, "as long as Michael Jordan is in the car." Police finally moved her.

Jordan's 1985–86 season was curtailed by a broken foot, but the way in which he reacted to the injury again showed his independence and ever-present desire to compete. On October 29, 1985, in only the third game of the regular season, Jordan fractured his left navicular tarsal bone, which supports and stabilizes the ankle and foot. He remained in a walking cast until January 22, 1986, and he did not play again until March 15, 1986.

The Bulls lost 43 of the 64 games they played during the four and one-half months Jordan was out. By mid-March, the Bulls' chance of winning a spot in the play-offs was diminishing. Not only had Jordan been absent, but the Bulls' two best centers had also missed a total of 45 games.

Jordan said of those few months spent in recovery that nothing in his life "comes close to being as depressing." He had lived a seemingly charmed life until that October day in 1985—he had never been seriously injured in high school or college or as a rookie pro.

"Basketball took a lot of my life and I [now] had nothing to spend my time on," Jordan said. "Basketball was a year-round, daily habit with me." When he wanted to resume that habit in March, however, he faced many objections. Bulls' president Jerry Reinsdorf and others felt his return wasn't worth the risk of hurting the foot again.

Jordan was told at a meeting three days before he came back that he risked re-injury and spending four to six months in another recovery effort. The team's general manager, its physician, and two orthopedic specialists also advised against return.

Not worried about re-injury, however, Jordan was determined to play. He had felt ready for nearly a month. Back in Chapel Hill, against doctors' advice, he had started working out again at the University of North Carolina. Jordan's insistence and a discussion with doctors led the Bulls' management to relent and in mid-March, they allowed Jordan to resume play.

After all the conflict, Jordan returned to action in a home game against the Milwaukee Bucks. Bulls' general manager Jerry Krause had instructed coach Albeck not to let Jordan play more than seven minutes in each half. He scored a total of 12 points during the game—accomplished by playing less than six minutes at the end of the second quarter and just under seven minutes at the start of the final period.

Even with Jordan back, the Bulls continued to lose. Jordan was chafing under the 14-minutes-a-game limit to which he had agreed. He urged the team to let him play full time. Jordan got his wish. He began playing for most of the game. In 15 games, he averaged over 20 points a game. He sparked the Bulls to six victories in nine games at the end of the year. A two-point win over Washington, before a crowd of almost 19,000 at Chicago Stadium, clinched a spot for the Bulls in the play-offs.

Entering the play-offs in the spring of 1986 set the stage for Jordan's spectacular, though brief, post-season effort. Jordan put on a brilliant offensive display for fans throughout the country in the second game of a best-of-five series against the Celtics. On April 20, in a nationally televised Sunday afternoon contest, he scored 63 points—an NBA single-game play-off record —breaking Elgin Baylor's record of 61 points, which had stood for 24 years. Despite Jordan's 63 points, the Celtics eventually won the game, 135-131.

A broken bone caused Jordan to miss 64 games in the 1985-86 season, leaving a large void in his daily life.

In the 18 regular-season games in which he played in 1985-86, Jordan made almost 46 percent of his field-goal attempts and 84 percent of his free throws, and he averaged 22.7 points per game. He scored a total of 408 points with 64 rebounds and 53 assists.

In the fall of 1986, Jordan started where he had left off in Boston the previous spring. His foot healed, he scored 50 points in a 108-103 victory in the season opener against the Knicks in New York. In the ninth game of the season, Jordan scored the Bulls' final 18 points in a two-point win over New York at Chicago Stadium, setting an NBA record for consecutive points. In the Bulls' first 20 games, Jordan led the team in scoring with 40 or more points in nine straight games.

"It's nice to have a nuclear weapon on your team," said Doug Collins, who was then the head coach of the Bulls—the third man to fill that spot in Jordan's career with Chicago. Jordan, meanwhile, said modestly that he was not "trying to go out and average as many points as I'm getting. I play the way the team wants me to play. The shots will come either for me or my teammates."

After his explosion in the play-offs the previous spring, Jordan knew other teams would try to tighten their defenses against him. But an expert player like Jordan defies most defensive tactics. After watching Jordan score 40 points against his team, New York

Knicks' coach Hubie Brown said that Jordan "single-handedly beat our traps all night long."

Jordan, "a nuclear weapon"!

The Celtics' Larry Bird said that Jordan was "going to get his points, no matter what." Jordan said of his high point totals, "I like playing the game. I don't treat it as pressure. I don't treat all this scoring as something that's going to happen every day. I know I'm going to have some bad nights, and I'm also going to have some better nights."

He had quite a few of the better nights in 1986–87. Jordan's high scoring didn't stop. He also played in all of Chicago's 82 regular-season games. Jordan's per game average of 37.1 points was 8.1 points better than that of runner-up Dominique Wilkins of Atlanta. During the 1986–87 season, Jordan made 48 percent of his field-goal attempts and almost 86 percent of his free-throw attempts. His 2.88 steals per game was second in the NBA. He also had 430 rebounds, 377 assists, and almost twice as many blocked shots as any other teammate. At a game in Pontiac, Michigan, on March 4, 1987, he scored 61 points.

That game made Jordan the third player in history to score more than 58 points in a game more than once. The other two were Wilt Chamberlain and Elgin Baylor. Five weeks later, on April 16, Jordan again scored 61 points, topping the magical 3,000-point mark. With this second 61-point game of the season he became the only player other than Chamberlain ever to score 50 or more points in three consecutive games. He had scored 50 in Milwaukee on April 13

Wilt Chamberlain, the 7-footer who played in the NBA over 3 decades, holds a host of all-time scoring records including the one for the most consecutive games (7) with 50-or-more points.

and 53 at home against Indiana on April 12.

NBA fans throughout the country loved Jordan. By the 1986–87 season, attendance at Bulls' games averaged almost 16,000, a Chicago Stadium record. In one stretch of 12 home and away games, the Bulls played before 10 sellout crowds.

The Bulls' 1986–87 regular-season record put them in the play-offs. Again, they faced Boston in the first round, and the Celtics won, ending Jordan's third season with the Bulls. After playing only a little more than two full seasons, Jordan was an established star.

Jordan with some of his fans.

# 5

## *Sharing His Success*

Jordan has traveled a long way from his days as an unpopular teenager. Today, everyone from the youngster on the playground to the corporate executive is attracted to him. His friends say Jordan's easy smile and outgoing manner please people. Off the basketball court, Jordan shows a caring, compassionate, sensitive side of himself. "Certain people have that charisma, full of life and all," coach Collins said. "He's like a magnet. Wherever he goes, he draws people."

One reporter found "a lot of little kid inside that 6-foot, 6-inch body. At times, he seems naive as he wanders about the world." Jordan has often displayed his affection for people, especially children. For example, at a NCAA play-off game in New Orleans in 1982, a streetwise 11-year-old boy talked his way onto the floor during the game and ended up sitting on Jordan's lap. Jordan developed a friendship with the boy, exchanging letters and telephone calls.

While visiting a children's hospital one day, Jordan wrote a check for a donation of $15,000. On Halloween in 1986, the Bulls were playing in New York, so Jordan taped a message on the front door of his townhouse: "Sorry I missed you. If you want trick or treat, come back in three days. Michael Jordan."

Such a considerate gesture is uncommon. Some professional athletes avoid fan contact, and a few even refuse to talk to reporters. Not Jordan—he goes out of his way to answer their questions. Since his first days as a pro, Jordan was a media sensation. As the Bulls moved from city to city in the fall of 1984, the press stalked the rookie. Although some people who knew Jordan said he tired of the same questions, he didn't show it when he was with the news media. He knew that how he answered those questions would make up the image he presented to the public.

Jordan is patient with the media and fans, he says, because "basketball—all my fans—they have given a lot to me. This is my way of giving something back to the community. I'll always remember when I wasn't so popular."

Today, Jordan is extremely popular. His appeal allows him to do product endorsements and promotions, such as television commercials—which can be very lucrative. Jordan employs a Washington, D.C.-

based management group to watch over his financial interests. They carefully screen companies that want to use Jordan to promote their products and try to maintain the former United States Olympic star's all-American image. His major commercial contract is for Nike's Air Jordan line of shoes and clothing.

Despite the intensity level at which the game is played, Jordan exhibits a calm poise on the basketball court.

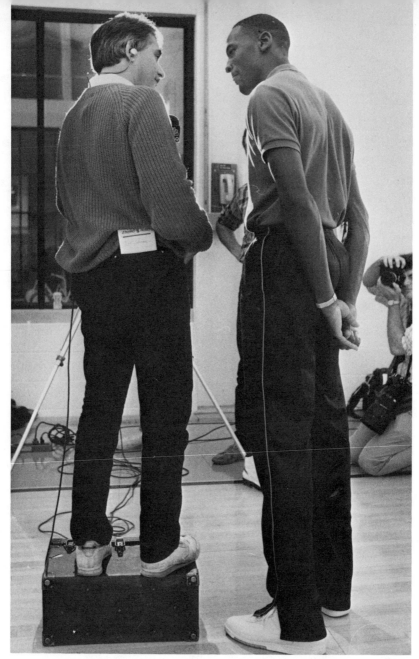

Jordan readily cooperates with the media.

Jordan's seven-year, $6.3 million contract with the Bulls will eventually pay him $1 million a year to play basketball. With his additional income from endorsements, royalties, and appearance fees, Jordan's yearly income is said to be near $2 million.

Jordan's management group also arranges for him to appear at charities and in public service campaigns, which give Jordan additional media exposure. For example, he spent one morning with children afflicted with Down's syndrome while filming an NBA-sponsored commercial for the Special Olympics. Even though he is aware that these appearances contribute to his marketing image, Jordan is dedicated to such activities and genuinely loves children.

Another time, the Bulls were waiting for a late flight at Chicago's O'Hare Airport. A large group of college students recognized Jordan and soon engulfed him, asking for autographs. An airline clerk noticed the commotion and offered to take him to a private office. But Jordan refused the chance to escape and continued to sign autographs and pose for photographs.

In 1986, Jordan's agent, David Falk, said that Jordan—then 23 years old—was "financially set for life." But as Jordan's performance remains strong and his appeal to fans continues to grow, several more years of playing basketball seem to be ahead for him.

In the 1987-1988 season, Jordan was named NBA Most Valuable Player and NBA Defensive Player of

Jordan rises...

...above all competition.

the Year. He played his fifth All-Star game, and he was named the All-Star Game Most Valuable Player.

While the 1987-1988 season was his year for awards, 1989-1990 was Jordan's year for shattering records. He led the league in scoring for the fourth straight year in 1990, and he became the Bulls' all-time point total leader, passing Bob Love's record of 12,623 points. Jordan also scored his career high of 69 points this season, in a 117-113 overtime victory in Cleveland on March 28.

Once again, however, the Detroit Pistons eliminated the Bulls on the way to the championship—for the third year straight. They stopped the Bulls in the Eastern Conference finals, this time in 7 games.

Jordan readily admits that he would love to win an NBA championship. "But if I don't, he says, "I'll walk away with my head held high. I've made a name for myself and earned the respect of my peers, and that can be far greater than any championship."

With or without a championship, Michael Jordan is basketball's favorite celebrity. He draws the crowds to the basketball arena and to their television sets, where he's a favorite guest of "The Arsenio Hall Show" and "Late Night with David Letterman."

Jordan likes expensive clothes and wears Italian suits to business meetings. His overall lifestyle is more practical than wild, however. Chicago Chevrolet dealers had offered him his pick of cars to drive. Instead of a flashy Corvette, Jordan chose a truck because, he said, it would be useful in Chicago's snowstorms.

When the snow stops, Jordan heads for the golf course. He began playing in college, where he became friends with Davis Love III, now on the Professional Golfers' Association Tour. Love gave Jordan his first new set of clubs—with special built-in grips for Jordan's large hands.

Since college, the competitive Jordan has improved his golf game considerably. During the off-season in the summer of 1986, Jordan couldn't run because of the foot he had broken the previous fall. But he could, and did, play golf to stay in shape. Now Jordan tells reporters that he might play professional golf after he quits basketball.

Can he play too much basketball? Jordan doesn't think so—it's a 12-month passion for him. "I don't think I'll ever lose my enthusiasm," he has said. "I love the game of basketball."

# MICHAEL JORDAN'S BASKETBALL STATISTICS

*University of North Carolina*

| YEAR | GAMES PLAYED | FIELD GOALS Attempted/Made | % | FREE THROWS Attempted/Made | % |
|---|---|---|---|---|---|
| 1981-82 | 34 | 358/191 | .534 | 108/78 | .722 |
| 1982-83 | 36 | 527/282 | .535 | 167/123 | .737 |
| 1983-84 | 31 | 448/247 | .551 | 145/113 | .779 |
| Totals | 101 | 1,333/720 | .540 | 420/314 | .748 |

*Chicago Bulls—Regular Season*

| YEAR | GAMES PLAYED | FIELD GOALS Attempted/Made | % | FREE THROWS Attempted/Made | % |
|---|---|---|---|---|---|
| 1984-85 | 82 | 1,625/837 | .515 | 746/630 | .845 |
| 1985-86 | 18 | 328/150 | .457 | 125/105 | .840 |
| 1986-87 | 82 | 2,279/1,098 | .482 | 972/833 | .857 |
| 1987-88 | 82 | 1,998/1,069 | .535 | 860/723 | .841 |
| 1988-89 | 81 | 1,795/966 | .538 | 793/674 | .850 |
| 1989-90 | 82 | 1,964/1,034 | .526 | 699/593 | .848 |
| Totals | 427 | 9,989/5,154 | .516 | 4,195/3,558 | .848 |

*NBA Play-offs*

| YEAR | GAMES PLAYED | FIELD GOALS Attempted/Made | % | FREE THROWS Attempted/Made | % |
|---|---|---|---|---|---|
| 1984-85 | 4 | 78/34 | .436 | 58/48 | .828 |
| 1985-86 | 3 | 95/48 | .505 | 39/34 | .872 |
| 1986-87 | 3 | 84/35 | .417 | 39/35 | .897 |
| 1987-88 | 10 | 260/138 | .531 | 99/86 | .869 |
| 1988-89 | 17 | 390/199 | .510 | 229/183 | .799 |
| 1989-90 | 16 | 426/219 | .514 | 159/133 | .836 |
| Totals | 53 | 1,333/673 | .505 | 623/519 | .833 |

1985   Rookie of the Year; NBA All-Rookie Team; Schick Pivotal Player Award
1986   NBA record-holder of most points in playoff game—63—against Boston on April 20, 1986
1987   All-NBA First Team; led NBA in scoring
1988   NBA Most Valuable Player; NBA Defensive Player of the Year; All-NBA First Team; First Team Most Valuable Player; NBA All-Star Game Most Valuable Player; led NBA in scoring; led NBA in steals

| REBOUNDS | POINTS | AVERAGE |
|---|---|---|
| 149 | 460 | 13.5 |
| 197 | 721 | 20.0 |
| 163 | 607 | 19.6 |
| 509 | 1,788 | 17.7 |

| REBOUNDS Offensive/Defensive | TOTAL | ASSISTS | PERSONAL FOULS | STEALS | BLOCKED SHOTS | POINTS | AVERAGE |
|---|---|---|---|---|---|---|---|
| 167/367 | 534 | 481 | 285 | 196 | 69 | 2,313 | 28.2 |
| 23/41 | 64 | 53 | 46 | 37 | 21 | 408 | 22.7 |
| 166/264 | 430 | 377 | 237 | 236 | 125 | 3,041 | 37.1 |
| 139/310 | 449 | 485 | 270 | 259 | 131 | 2,868 | 35.0 |
| 149/503 | 652 | 650 | 247 | 234 | 65 | 2,633 | 32.5 |
| 143/422 | 565 | 519 | 241 | 227 | 54 | 2,753 | 33.6 |
| 787/1,907 | 2,694 | 2,565 | 1,326 | 1,189 | 465 | 14,016 | 32.8 |

| REBOUNDS Offensive/Defensive | TOTAL | ASSISTS | PERSONAL FOULS | STEALS | BLOCKED SHOTS | POINTS | AVERAGE |
|---|---|---|---|---|---|---|---|
| 7/16 | 23 | 34 | 15 | 11 | 4 | 117 | 29.3 |
| 5/14 | 19 | 17 | 13 | 7 | 4 | 131 | 43.7 |
| 7/14 | 21 | 18 | 11 | 6 | 7 | 107 | 35.7 |
| 23/48 | 71 | 47 | 38 | 24 | 11 | 363 | 36.3 |
| 26/93 | 119 | 130 | 65 | 42 | 13 | 591 | 34.8 |
| 24/91 | 115 | 109 | 54 | 45 | 14 | 587 | 36.7 |
| 92/276 | 368 | 355 | 196 | 135 | 53 | 1,896 | 35.8 |

1989    All-NBA First Team; NBA All-Defensive First Team; Schick Pivotal Player Award; led NBA in scoring

1990    Bulls' all-time point total leader; led NBA in scoring; led NBA in steals

## ACKNOWLEDGEMENTS

The photographs are reproduced through the courtesy of: Christopher Lauber, pp. 1, 9, 12, 14, 47; Jonathan Daniel Photography, pp. 2, 6, 10, 15, 19, 23, 26, 31, 32, 39, 41, 50 (top and bottom), 53, 56; Office of Sports Information, University of North Carolina, p. 20; Chicago Sun-Times, pp. 44, 48; New York Knickerbockers, p. 34; National Basketball Association, p. 43.
Front cover: Christopher Lauber. Back cover: John E. Biever.

EAU CLAIRE PUBLIC LIBRARY

EAU CLAIRE DISTRICT LIBRARY